MIND BALANCING THROUGH MEDITATION

(BASED ON BHAGAVAD GITA CHAPTER-6)

DR. JAGADEESH PILLAI

|| DEDICATED TO ALL BHAGAVAD GITA LOVERS ACROSS THE GLOBE ||

Contents

Prayer

HARE RAMA HARE RAMA, RAMA RAMA HARE HARE
- HARE KRISHNA, HARE KRISHNA, KRISHNA
KRISHNA, HARE HARE

(Mantra - Kali Santaranopanishad)

About The Author

Dr. Jagadeesh Pillai a voracious reader, Four Times Guinness World Record holder, writer, and true research scholar was born in Varanasi, the abode of Lord Shiva. He is Ph.D. in Vedic Science. He is a multi-faceted polymath with innate qualities, creative ideas and many remarkable achievements. Although his roots extend back to "Gods own Country"(Kerala), the residents of Varanasi feel proud of him and adore him as a child of Varanasi who caters to every individual in need without any expectations. A deep study into his profile reflects that he has added so many feathers to his cap which makes him quite unique. He is a four times Guinness Book of World Records Holder in the following subjects :

"Script to Screen" which he achieved by producing and directing a state of art animation film within the shortest time possible by breaking the earlier set record by Canadians. There are many national and international Awards and Recognitions to his credit.

Longest Line of Post Cards which he has done on the occasion of 163 years of Indian Postal Day by 16300 post cards. The event was also connected with a questionnaire about Indian Flag.

Largest Poster Awareness Campaign – This was achieved by designing an awareness campaign on the subject "Beti Bachao – Beti Padhao".

Largest Envelop – Towards tribute to Prime Minister's initiative 'Make in India' – he has created about 4000 sq meter envelop using waste papers.

Attempted by lighting 70000 candles on a 210 kg cake to celebrate the 70th Indian Independence day recorded in World Records India.

Attempted a documentary on Dhamek Stupa of Sarnath dubbing in 17 languages, result is waiting from Guinness World Records.

He is versatile in Gita teaching. The young generation is fond of his Gita teaching and he has changed the life of many young through his continued motivational boost up and teachings.

He has composed and sung Gayatri Mantra in 1000 different tunes.

He has composed and sung Hanuman Chalisa in 108 different tunes.

He has composed and sung hundreds of Sanskrit Bhajans, Patriotic songs, etc.

He has written and directed so many short films and documentaries for awareness campaigns.

He has done voluntary services to UP Police and Kerala Police to spread awareness campaigns on the various issue through videos and photography.

He is on the path of authoring thousands of books on Indian culture, Indian Temples, and the life of extraordinary people.

It is hard to believe that he has produced and directed more than 100 Documentaries on a particular city (Varanasi) which is done by a single person.

He has helped and guided more than 25 boys and girls to achieve world records through various creative and innovative methods.

A multifaceted person who can apply the best of his intellect using the God-given blessings which have been showered upon every human being granting them an immense capacity to learn, experience, and experiment with many things and do wonders in this world of discrimination and disparities.

He is a teacher and a student at the same time who always learns every day and teaches every day. As a master, his weakness was that he never sticks to a particular subject. Perhaps this weakness gives him the strength to master any area which he came across.

Each of his days dawned with learning a new topic and he spend most of his time experimenting and researching it.

He is also a selfless social activist and a motivational speaker.

His life was full of struggle, ups and downs, and failures. But he never gave up and faced all his trials and tribulations full of confidence. Today he is a successful young man with a lot of enthusiasm and rich life experience.

He has sung full Ram Charita Manas 51 hours audio by his own composition. He has also sung the whole Bhagavad-Gita in his own composition with a rhythmic background.

He has also sung "Lokah Samastha Sukhino Bhavantu" in 50 different languages.

Currently working on a detailed and scientific study on Veda, Upanishad, Puranas, Bhagavad Gita, etc.

Currently, he is the Hon' Chancellor of 'Eurasia Digital University'.

Awards

Four Times Guinness World Records

Winner of Mahatma Gandhi Vishwa Shanti Puraskar

Mahatma Gandhi Global Peace Ambassador
Kashi Ratna Award

Dr. APJ Abdul Kalam Motivational Person of the Year 2017

Mother Teresa Award

Indira Gandhi Priyadarshini Award

Bharat Vikas Ratna Award

Udyog Ratna Award

Vigyan Prasar Award

Poorvanchal Ratn Samman

Preface

MEDITATION, CONCENTRATION, BEING DEAF, BEING BLIND, BEAING SENSE LESS, BEING ACTION LESS, MENTAL BALANCING, ACHIEVING STABLE MENTALITY, ETC.

Three things are important to achieve the above state of mind.

1. Concentrate the feeling of mind whatever we do.

2. Limitated lifestyle *(fulfil only the required necessities)*

3. Equality in everything *(everything is of the Supreme)*

In this book Krishna lights up the route to achieve 'Qualified Soul" status.

MIND BALANCING THROUGH MEDITATION

In this book based on Bhagavad Gita chapter-6, Krishna lights up the route towards to achieve the 'Qualified Soul" status.

From the f previous chapter we have learned that one can qualify his mind by removing the "I did" thought from whatever karma he does. Instead, he submits and dedicates all of his actions towards his duty to the Supreme like a servant does his duties assigned to him by his master. Here the master is Krishna and we all are his servants.

Eg: A father says I did it for my son.

There is strong bondage between a father & his son and the father thinks that he is the master/owner or the authority of his son.

But for the Supreme, the father and his son both are two humans only, because the master and the ultimate authority of both humans are the Supreme. Father is just a temporary caretaker and the son is just a newcomer on the earth.

Father has to _take care (action)_ his son because he has more life experiences and it is his _obligatory duty_ too, to help other human beings even if he is a son or not.

So, we all are doing our duty of taking care of other beings like our own son, daughter, spouse, brother, sister, etc. But the master/owner and authority of all the humans and other creatures like animals, birds, trees, land, mountains, etc. are the Supreme.

We also have to perform various other obligatory duties which are essential for the well being of other beings and the existence of the earth.

But by ignorance, the father forgets that the real owner of all humans is the Supreme (Krishna) and thus he develops false bondage and attachment with his son. He believes that he is the owner/master and the only authority of his son and wealth whatever he possesses.

But the real owner of everything on the earth is the Supreme. We are just a temporary caretaker of some people, money and property.

For us and the Supreme, our existence and well-being of all humans are important.

For us, our well-being means, having good food, enjoy life, lavish, luxury, fulfill various desires, develop bondage and attachment with physical and material things and live in a false belief that we owns this, that, etc.

When the Supreme gave you the birth on the land, everything needed for your survival was also given like a Boss of the company sends one of the employees for a business tour to Australia, he gives you a return flight ticket, provides food & accommodation, salary, and other perks, etc.

Let's compare :

Your birth on earth Employee landed in Australia

I own a father - I am the Boss here

I own a house - I own the hotel

I enjoy food, etc. - Enough food for me

I enjoy the beauty of nature - I am here to enjoy

I am happy and perfect - I am happy and perfect

But why did the Supreme or the Boss sent you

has sent you

(to do his duties) (to do his duties)

You forget the Supreme You forget your Boss

and the duties to be performed enjoying your days in

and becoming ignorant Australia and making the

Boss fool.

Your actual duty was You forget the duties

To do selfless karma, assigned to you by

fight with situations and your boss. Instead you

make mental balance, enjoys everything

detach from desires,

attachments, love

to all beings, forgive

other's actions done by

ignorance of guna

dominance.

HUMAN'S DUTY WAS EMPLOYEE'S DUTY WAS

To qualify as a Great Soul You have to report to your

by purifying the Mind and Boss, per your performance

senses by doing various you will be given promotion

actions to satisfy Krishna and chances to become a

or to become like Krishna boss

(various adverse situations

has to face, chase and

overcome to qualify)

But you are disqualified But you are disqualified, so the

so the Supreme Boss, terminated you from

destroyed your body the company.

and taken back the Soul

and send to other location

for further development.

You were temporary here You were just an employee

as a servant of in the company, not the Boss.

the Supreme

The Supreme has nothing The Boss has nothing to

to do with your relationship do with your family's well

with physical and material being and won't even think

things, because you were about them after your.

a caretake not was the termination

owner.

The Supreme will send your You will search for new

Soul to different bodies at a job and maybe change

different locations to clean many jobs to become

the mind and senses by a perfect employee

fighting with life situations and later to achieve

Boss quality

So, what are mentioned above in bold letters are the main purpose of taking birth on earth. But we forget that so we need to take more and more births to qualify.

Krishna wants to create more humans with Krishna's quality like a father wants his son to become a father with his qualities after marriage.

So to bring up the Soul, the scattered mind which are attracted to various false physical and material desires to be cleaned and to fill with selfless desire to perform the obligatory duties which are assigned by the Supreme.

So, this chapter is going to teach how to concentrate and bring back the scattered mind and senses to a peaceful atmosphere to purify it through meditation.

***

This chapter teaches us various methods to be within in your soul by concentrating your mind and controlling your senses.

In another words, it will teache us :

MEDITATION, CONCENTRATION, BEING DEAF, BEING BLIND, BEAING SENSE LESS, BEING ACTION LESS

(Remember the three donkey's of Mahatma Gandhi)

Still there are lot of confusion about Karma (action), what exactly it is and how it affects and disturb our mind. Most people has a belief that what we do by hand or legs are the actions (karma).

Action actually emerges in the mind through thoughts, feelings, imagination, while listening, while visualising, while expecting, while desiring etc. and it reflects outside either through hand, leg, mouth, eyes, ear, etc.

Lets see a list of **actions (karma)** happens in mind :

Pain, anger, feeling of revenge, frustrations, confusions, doubts, suspicion, disappointment, despondency, distress, superiority complex, inferiority complex, ego, emotional, sentimental, feeling of "I am", "I" own this, "my" house, "my" land, "my" property, "I" did, "I" lost, he won, "I" am good, he is bad, "my" caste is good, his caste is bad, he is poor, "I am" rich, his religion is bad, my religion is good, he is not accepting me, he cheated/deceived me, "I" cheated him/her, "I" will kill him, "I" killed him, "my" father/mother/spouse/sibilings/friend is expired, "I" hate them, "I" want to spoil him/her, he/she is not loving me, many kind of bad imaginations, checking other's privacy, reading unethical books, "I" am not successful, "I am" so successful, over happiness, abusing, quarrel, fighting, "I" loved him/her, he/she left me, he/she disconnected me, that country is not good, that minister is not good, my city is not good, my neighbour is not good, "I" have problems, expecting publicity by doing services, self praising, expecting appreciation, "I am" the master, "I am" the owner, "I am" talented, laziness, interfering in other's work, intevenening in other's matter, disturbing somebody, over expectation, over smartness, etc. and the opposite of all above are also actions.

The most important villain is

"I", "I am", "I own", "my", "my own"

Infact, everything <u>owns</u> by the Supreme, even the "I", because as mentioned above, we are a temporary visitor on the earth and a temporary caretaker of few things, not the owners.

Let's go through a conversation I had with an old friend, a medical professional, who is currently settled in the US with his family and kids since last 20 years. He was a native of Kerala (India) and born and brought up there.

During the 21 days lockdown period in India, oneday, he called me from the US (he was calling me after five years) to enquire about the situation here in India. But just in few seconds he continuesly talked about the short comings of Indian medical system, shortcomings of actions taken by Indian Government and so many other desparities about India. He was totally frustrated to see so many things about India through media. More than half an hour he talked and I just heard all that with a silent mode. Atlast, he even confessed and said that he called me to share his frustration.

Before cutting the phone, I just asked few questions.

Where are you now? – In the US with family and kids.

Is there any plan to come back to India after retirement ?

No. we got citizenship here, our kids are born and brought up here so no way that we will come back and settle in India, but will be coming occasionaly on vacations, that's all.

Then I asked..

Why are you worrying about India?

Phone cut !

A bundle of frustrations he has shared on me like somebody throws their garbage on other's home.

If it was somebody else in my place, they might be discussing for more than two hours about various issues in India.

Why and who has said to do that?

These are called actually *actions*.

Instead of thinking about the issues in the US and in his family there, he is un-necessarily concentrating and watching the issues and shortcoming of India.

All these actions are happening in his mind.

Things to note :

Action No. 1 – his _un-necessary thinking_ about India

Action No. 2 - _Calling to India_ and _sharing_ bad thoughts it to other

Person

Action No. 3 – Person in India _attending_ and _listening_ to his call

Action No.4 – The person in India _silently listening_ with a balanced

mind and not allowing to make any effect on his

mind, so his mind is cool.

Eight kind of actions are happened here - (1) un-necessary thinking, (2) calling to India, (3) sharing, (4) bad thoughts, (5) call attending, (6) listening, (7) silently listening with a (8) balanced mind and (9) wasting time.

Let me clarify 5 to 9 actions...

(5) Indian person attend the call..

(6) Started listening (but in few second understood that his talking are of no use) but

(7) Silently listening like a deaf (mode of listening has changed)

(8) Mind balancing when call was for more than 10-15 mintutes

(9) Both have wasted time.

The US person is like a patient of frustruation.

The Indian person intelligently managed it with a cool mind, so no effect on his mind. To give respect to the other person who was calling after five years, he was just listening like a deaf.

It was like one person was throwing a garbage, but the other person has not catched, touched and accepted it (escaped from affecting his mind).

We have to learn from the above that we will have to face such many situations in life, but at the same time we have to concentrate while doing every karma that it should not make any bad effect on our mind. It won't be easy to escape from the karmas and that's why it was not possible for the Indian person to attend the call of his friend from US. He is unaware that for what the US person is calling. While attending the call, in few seconds, he understood that the US person is speaking something unwanted and not good for the mind. But to respect his call, instead of responding and accepting his frustrations, he turned him into "silent mode or meditative mode". The US Person was speaking a lot, but the Indian person closed his door of mind until he finish it.

Such hundreds of incidents will come our way everyday and every minute, but if we carefully concentrate on every action, we can clean and win our mind. From a clean mind, wise decisions, ideas, intellIgence etc. comes up and we can also be saved from many unwanted tensions and other happenings in life.

***

So, this chapter is about

MEDITATION, CONCENTRATION, BEING DEAF, BEING BLIND, BEAING SENSE LESS, BEING ACTION LESS, MENTAL BALANCING, ACHIEVING STABLE MENTALITY, ETC.

Three things are important to achieve the above state of mind.

1. Concentrate the feeling of mind whatever we do.

2. Limitated lifestyle (fulfil only the required necessities)

3. Equality in everything *(everything is of the Supreme)*

Remember the school days when the teacher has told us to memorise an essay and write it on an exam next week. Few students will memorise the essay word to word as it is by hundred times repeatition without understanding the subject in detail. But some students won't memorise it, instead, they will try to understand the subject in detail by concentrating the points mentioned in it. So when they have to write it in an exam, they don't need to write the essay as it is, but they can write it in their own understanding, may be even better than the original.

***

Whoever does actions towards obligatory duty to the Supreme, without expecting the fruit of it, will be called as a "Qualified Soul" and then he itself later becomes a "Qualified to renunciate Action". Nobody can become a "Qualified Soul" by stopping/escaping from the society by avoiding the actions (face & fight) he has to do and nobody can "Qualify to renunciate Action" without complete purification/renunciation of all actions.

Qualified Soul – (He does, but sacrificing the fruit)

Qualified to renunciate action – (Neither he does, nor the fruit)

(Complete cleaning/purification/detachment required by the fire of sacrifice to become "Qualified to renunciate action") 1-2/6

***

The person who are about to become a "Qualified Soul", will continuesly practise to achieve the status by doing a lot of selfless social service, mind balancing, sacrifices etc.

and once he has achieved it, he will try to maintain it by self mastry by inner renunciation and steady practise (Sadhna). Earlier the person was living for his family with possession and possessiveness, but once he has realised the obligatory duties to be done towards the Supreme, he starts doing various selfless services to the society without expecting the fruit of it. Earlier it will be difficult, many consequences has to face from the family and other people who are still attached with the worldly pleasures. But the wisdom and development happened to him won't allow him to re-involve in that selfish kind of living. People will oppose, they will try to pull his leg, will blame him, will say that he is detaching connections with the family etc. Earlier he was sticked with some relations as his own, but later he disconnected now believing that the whole world as his family. Then the field of his action will change/expand from "for the family only" to "for every other being in the world." For him, it is his spiritual development to next level, but for others he becomes a wrong person. His social involvement and connections with lot of people, etc. wont be affordable/acceptable by his family. Once he has broken the wall of limitations, he need to practise not to break the mind. 3-4/6.

Eg : We learned driving, but if we won't practise it, no perfection is

possible.

***

Many arrows of allegations, objections, rejections, blames, abuses, condemnations from family and outsiders will be coming to disturb your mind. But we have to face it all by not allowing it to make an effect on your mind. You have to make your mind more and more strong to win every situation so that you can reap good results out of it. A strong and purified mind will work like a friend and it will help you to develop intelligence, wisdom, ideas, talents, etc.

But by chance, if the arrows of above hits your mind, the effect of it will work like an enemy for you. Your mental stability will down, you will stop selfless services you were doing, you will cry, become anger, feeling of revenge will develop, laziness will develop, suicidal feelings will develop, fear of loss will develop, you will spoil you and others, all of your capabilities, talents, etc. will be down and finally you will collapse.

A strong mind of you = Your friend

A weak mind of you = Your enemy

Various situations of life when mind becomes 'weak - enemy' :

1. Boyfriend/Girlfriend break up.

2. Somebody close to you is expired.

3. Somebody continuesly abusing/condemning/blaming you.

4. Financial Problems/debts etc.

5. Not meeting the expectation of spouse

6. Parents are weak, because their children not bringing the

expected grade in class.

7. Neighbour's prosperous.

8. Permanent health problem of a person in the family.

9. A child who born with desparities.

10. Mother-in-law problems

11. Brother, Sister, Brother-in-law, sister-in-law problems.

12. If you are doing something very good, other's jealousy will harm

your mind.

13. Inferiority/Superiority complex .

14. Office promotion issue.

15. Boss not good.

16. Job is very tight, salary is not satisfactory.

17. Unable to meet/satisfy all needs of family

18. Roomate's attitude

19. People will hate you.

20. Issues because of caste or creed, etc. etc.

It clarify that our life is actually the WAR and our MIND is the BATTLEFIELD. The above are the arrows we regularly face in our life to sustain and survive.

If we closely look into the face of the people around us, we can imagine that most of their minds are affected with any one of the above issue.

Facing a real war is more easy than facing the war of life. A war lasts for few months or few years and if we are not a good warrior, we will finish there.

But the war of life is hundred times tougher than the real war. It starts the day we born and it last approx. 70 to 80 years until we die. But for the soul, it is not fixed because it has to take many more births to continue the fight to win/purify/clean the mind and join the Supreme.

But a clear/strong/perfect mind will help you to expand any level and do wonders in the world.

Dr. APJ Abdul Kalam, Pandit Madan Mohan Malviya, Swami Vivekananda, Mahatma Gandhi, Dr. Sarveppalli Radhakrishnan, Vinoba Bhaveji, Sardar Vallabhai Patel, Sri Aurobindo, Albert Einsten and many scientists like him, Bill Gates, Steve Jobs, Ebraham Lincoln, etc. are few personalities who has expanded them with a lot of contributions to the world.

But the opposite to the above is, born, school/college, a small job or business for food and shelter, passing 24 hours being within a family, then instead of doing something more good or selfless service, they will enjoy their daily life, possess/secure maximum wealth they can, find shortcomings on others and it goes like that. Same like the birds and animals are living. They also born, find their food and shelter, sleeps at night, passing the days, one day they will also die. But they don't need education, no job, not developing additional intelligence, no school, hospital and temples for them and there is no opportunity for them to expand.

But humans only has the opportunity to expand them to any level. But the life of most of the people are limited to the life of birds and animals only. But the only extra thing the human does is, acquire some some wealth and relations etc., and then fight to feed, maintain and secure them. But the Supreme (the real owner of all of us) will take him back without an advance notice and without thinking about any of our attachment and possessions.

***

So the most important thing to manage is our MIND. Practise silence with a smile on face when ever there is any kind of adverse situations as listed above.

Its not every easy to control and achieve a stable mind. We need to extensively practise facing/overcoming various heart breaking/shocking situtations. In this book, you will get many options to practise and achieve the same. *(The ultimate secret still to reveal at 18/16).*

***

Nose Tip Focusing Meditation (Nasikagra Drishti)

Those who are facing the above adverse situations and fighting to get mental stability, need to practise the following meditation. Whenever it is possible, he need to find a quite, calm, clean place. No any kind of sound should be there in that area. Better to practise alone and early in the morning or late night when there is silence every where.

Sit straight in a comfortable meditative pose on the ground.

Look straight, relax, breath normally, relax the shoulders and place the palms on your knees, close your eyes, then try to open your eyes 1/10 and try to focus the tip of your nose very softly. Continue normal breating and sometime hold the breath to get more concentration. If you feel pain or discomfort, either open or close the eyes. Repeat it as many times as possible. After few days, you will be abel to practise it for longer duration and it will take the practitioner to higher state of consciousness during meditation. Keep the gaze very soft, sort of like looking, but not looking.

What science says ;

This the main purpose of this meditation is to cut the mind from the outside world and get full inward attention. While doing this meditation our root chakra will be activated and it also activate the frontial lobe part of the brain. If there is difficulty to focus directly on the nose tip, you can focus on your forefinger tip and bring it near to your nose tip. When the eyes are focused on the nose tip, the optic nerves between the eyebrow will also be active and it also balances the right and left hemispheres of the brain which will also help to concentrate the mind. Activation of pineal and pituitary glands during this meditation has the effect to kill the old habils, pain, agony, revenge etc. and makes the space to fill goodness into it.

There are various meditation techniques available around the world. But if somebody can practise atleast this one, they can control their mind from emotions, any kind of adverse situations, and can clear any kind of dirts by filling lot of peace within in it. (Rajasik guna will also come down when we practise the above)

***

Apart from the above meditation, we have to control our sleep, food, enjoyment and entertainments. Over sleep, less sleep, over food, less food, over enjoyment, less enjoyment , etc. will leads to disturb the health and a disturbed health will also become a reason to worry and again disturbance of mind.

Those who have a good practise of the above, they can manage their mind within a second when something adverse happens in their life like a flame of lamp is montionless in a windless room. They will feel weightlessness in the mind and body (feeling of absence of sensation of weight).

They will be able to balancing every situation in life. Many such occasions will come in life where between relations or between friends we have to balace many things to avoid un-necessary quarrel or any other issues.

Don't try to make any issue with somebody's actions. Try your maximum to stay away from such people and if you are forced to stay there, practice silence and mind balancing. Sometime such situations are also required to practise mind balancing.

An example:

Ten years ago when I purchased a land, before go for registration the measurement has to be done. The left side & right side of my land belongs to two government employees. There is already house in the backside, but left and right are plain lands.

The day of measurement, I already guessed that the two government employees of left and right side of my land might have taken leave from their job and will be staying there to check whether I am over measuring my land. So I haven't visited there instead I sent my staff and instructed him to take measurement of left and right side of the land per the satisfaction of those government employees who took leave to save few inches of land if I over measured it. While taking the measurement, first ask them, if it is right, when they say correct, leave an inch of land more from us and then fix the point. I don't want them to lose something instead let me earn something.

Here I have to balance three people. Myself (already decided not to be there since I don't want to worry about how much I got and how much I lost). They both should not have any issue with it.

So I already surrended, to balance three people including me and for a comfortable/tensionless land measurement.

Such many occasions will come in life where we have to balance the situation, balance the people and balance our mind. Un-necessary intervention in other's life, trying to check their secrets and privacy will also disturb our life.

***

It won't be possible for a doctor to perform his duty if he insists to treat the patients by checking their living history, habits, attitude, behavious, nature, etc. *(except the few things they are permitted to ask to find out the reason the disease)*. Is it possible for a doctor to insist that he won't treat people who often angry, who take alcohol, who abuse people, who are illiterate, who has pshycic problem, etc. No. A doctor is liable to perfom his own duties of treating people, he has nothing to do with a person's personal life and his life secrets.

A clean mind which is filled with compassion to everybody, love, mercy, forgiveness, gratefulness, submitting every action to the Supreme and always connected with the Suprme, feels ultimate mental peace and satisfaction. Such people do not generate more sins through bad karma and diminishes the old one by continues practise of mental balancing.

Such people will feel and experience that they are in everybody, and everybody is in them. They will feel like one soul in everywhere and all are connected to the Supreme like salt mixes in the water and camphor mixes with the fire of flame.

Eg : Will you be joking with a student of class 10 if he has done any immature mistake. The intelligent people, if by chance you are pursuing your PHD, will understand that you had also passed through that immature level (class 10) and this student will reach our level tomorrow. But to understand his mistakes we have to bring our mind to the level of that 10 class student.

Why parents forgive the mistakes of their kids, because they understand their limitations, immaturities which the parents also gone through in the past.

The Supeme will also help us when we are on the developing stage.

***

No every person can achieve the state of mental stability in on birth itself. It may take many births. Those who were already practising in previous birth, can continue practising in this birth also and they can even go and achieve higher level of it.

While practising the mental balancing & stability, if we leave the body in this birth, it will be continued next birth also from where we left practising in the previous birth. Apart from that we will get our new birth in a more upgraded location (rare opporutunity to born in a noble and wealthy family or in the family of scholars) so that we can easily achieve high level of mental balancing, achieve wisdom & intelligence and we can expand our level from common to extra ordinary.

In their new birth either at a noble family or in the family of scholars, they will realize about their karmas what they have followed in their previous birth and will continue to achieve higher level.

Various heart breaking problems will be wringing out our mind, if we try our best to fight, chase, face and overcome the situation by balancing the mind, we will gradually liberated from the problems one by one or we will achieve such a mental state to face any kind of problems without disturbing our mind.

When we face and overcome the adverse situations, a lot of our sins are also washing out which might have been generated by us in the previous birth or this birth. That's why in an earlier chapter it was said that for the effect of every problem there must be a cause.

Those qualified souls who fights, chase, face and overcome every adverse situations are considered as great in the eyes of the Supreme because only such person can do something for the existence of this world.

Before concluding this chaper, let's go through the following notes :

I am one human out of 779 homosapian species of the world. There are millions of other species are also there. So for the creator or the Supreme one human (i.e. me) out of millions of different speceies are not that important and if anything happens to me, it wont' affect any other homosapians or any other speceies.

There are two controlling agents in the nature to manage every species. They are called **"Predator & Prey"**. A predator is an organism that eats another organism and the prey is the organism which the predator eats. (An example of prey is a deer being hunted by a man).

Nature never disturb the equibilliarim either by destroying a particular speceies or increasing a lot of particular species. It will have a balancing. But only the humans are trying to disturb the equibilliarim.

There are small mammals, large mammlas, extreme wild animals like Lion, Tiger, etc. in the forest, but still the deers are surviving in the forest. This is because of the self regularization ability of the nature.

When we go to the zoo or a forest, we check that whether the deers are still there or not, we never check specifically that a particular deer is there or lost. We don't want to know about it. Even those take the animal census, they only check how many are there, how many lost, not check whether a particular one still exists or not. The total number is important, that's all.

The same for humans also. We humans has no control or power over the nature and its own duties. For the nature, we all are just humans, it won't count how many father, mother, sons and family are there.

It is our own interest only that we want to live here with our family. The same interest of deers in the forest are forced them to escape when some animals attack them. The nature always want some changes that's why there are options which can kills also.

In 1347, in Europe about 250 lac people was expired because of pleague (black death). Nature never check whether the people who has survived was belongs to which religious category and whom they worshipped.

Nature only counts and check, who was able to survive and survived. According to the principle of Darvin, only those will survive who aro qualified to survive. Only those deers can survive which can cleverly escaped from lions, tigers, fight-or-flight and survive. Other will be wiped off authomatically. It doen't depends which God we worship, which temples/church/mosque we go, how much money we spent for God, etc.

Our survival depends on how much we are fit to live, how much we are capabile to fight with the situations in life, fight with virus, fight with health etc.

Every person has to ask

Whether my immunity is perfect?

What are the measures I am applying to maintain my health.

Whether my good habits are good?

Whether my mental desires and attachments are good?

Am I eager to accumulate lot of wealth, saving etc.?

Am I carry jealousy, anger, feeling of revenge in mind?

Are my thoughts purified?

What is your spiritual status?

There are many pandemic situations already happened in the world and lost millions of lives. But the nature and the death never ever counts in which God you believe or which religion you possess. Only those people who are qualified survive will only be survived.

So let's us try to understand the rule of nature of the Supreme.

English text of Slokhas of Chapter-6 for Quick Reference

1

śhrī bhagavān uvācha
anāśhritaḥ karma-phalaṁ kāryaṁ karma karoti yaḥ
sa sannyāsī cha yogī cha na niragnir na chākriyaḥ

2

yaṁ sannyāsam iti prāhur yogaṁ taṁ viddhi pāṇḍava
na hyasannyasta-saṅkalpo yogī bhavati kaśhchana

3

ārurukṣhor muner yogaṁ karma kāraṇam uchyate
yogārūḍhasya tasyaiva śhamaḥ kāraṇam uchyate

4

yadā hi nendriyārtheṣhu na karmasv-anuṣhajjate
sarva-saṅkalpa-sannyāsī yogārūḍhas tadochyate

5

uddhared ātmanātmānaṁ nātmānam avasādayet
ātmaiva hyātmano bandhur ātmaiva ripur ātmanaḥ

6

bandhur ātmātmanas tasya yenātmaivātmanā jitaḥ
anātmanas tu śhatrutve vartetātmaiva śhatru-vat

7

jitātmanaḥ praśhāntasya paramātmā samāhitaḥ
śhītoṣhṇa-sukha-duḥkheṣhu tathā mānāpamānayoḥ

8

jñāna-vijñāna-tṛiptātmā kūṭa-stho vijitendriyaḥ
yukta ityuchyate yogī sama-loṣhṭāśhma-kāñchanaḥ

9

suhṛin-mitrāryudāsīna-madhyastha-dveṣhya-bandhuṣhu
sādhuṣhvapi cha pāpeṣhu sama-buddhir viśhiṣhyate

10

yogī yuñjīta satatam ātmānaṁ rahasi sthitaḥ
ekākī yata-chittātmā nirāśhīr aparigrahaḥ

11

śhuchau deśhe pratiṣhṭhāpya sthiram āsanam ātmanaḥ
nātyuchchhritaṁ nāti-nīchaṁ chailājina-kuśhottaram

12, 13

tatraikāgraṁ manaḥ kṛitvā yata-chittendriya-kriyaḥ
upaviśhyāsane yuñjyād yogam ātma-viśhuddhaye

samam kāya-śhiro-grīvam dhārayann achalam sthiraḥ
samprekṣhya nāsikāgram svam diśhaśh chānavalokayan

14

praśhāntātmā vigata-bhīr brahmachāri-vrate sthitaḥ
manaḥ sanyamya mach-chitto yukta āsīta mat-paraḥ

15

yuñjann evam sadātmānam yogī niyata-mānasaḥ
śhāntim nirvāṇa-paramām mat-sansthām adhigachchhati

16

nātyaśhnatastu yogo 'sti na chaikāntam anaśhnataḥ
na chāti-svapna-śhīlasya jāgrato naiva chārjuna

17

yuktāhāra-vihārasya yukta-cheṣhṭasya karmasu
yukta-svapnāvabodhasya yogo bhavati duḥkha-hā

18

yadā viniyatam chittam ātmanyevāvatiṣhṭhate
niḥspṛihaḥ sarva-kāmebhyo yukta ityuchyate tadā

19

yathā dīpo nivāta-stho neṅgate sopamā smṛitā
yogino yata-chittasya yuñjato yogam ātmanaḥ

20

yatroparamate chittaṁ niruddhaṁ yoga-sevayā
yatra chaivātmanātmānaṁ paśhyann ātmani tuṣhyati

21

yatroparamate chittaṁ niruddhaṁ yoga-sevayā
yatra chaivātmanātmānaṁ paśhyann ātmani tuṣhyati

22

yaṁ labdhvā chāparaṁ lābhaṁ manyate nādhikaṁ tataḥ
yasmin sthito na duḥkhena guruṇāpi vichālyate

23

taṁ vidyād duḥkha-sanyoga-viyogaṁ yogasaṅjñitam
sa niśhchayena yoktavyo yogo 'nirviṇṇa-chetasā

24, 25

saṅkalpa-prabhavān kāmāns tyaktvā sarvān aśheṣhataḥ
manasaivendriya-grāmaṁ viniyamya samantataḥ
śhanaiḥ śhanair uparamed buddhyā dhṛiti-gṛihītayā
ātma-sansthaṁ manaḥ kṛitvā na kiñchid api chintayet

26

yato yato niśhcharati manaśh chañchalam asthiram
tatas tato niyamyaitad ātmanyeva vaśhaṁ nayet

27

*praśhānta-manasaṁ hyenaṁ yoginaṁ sukham uttamam
upaiti śhānta-rajasaṁ brahma-bhūtam akalmaṣham*

28

*yuñjann evaṁ sadātmānaṁ yogī vigata-kalmaṣhaḥ
sukhena brahma-sansparśham atyantaṁ sukham aśhnute*

29

*sarva-bhūta-stham ātmānaṁ sarva-bhūtāni chātmani
īkṣhate yoga-yuktātmā sarvatra sama-darśhanaḥ*

30

*yo māṁ paśhyati sarvatra sarvaṁ cha mayi paśhyati
tasyāhaṁ na praṇaśhyāmi sa cha me na praṇaśhyati*

31

*sarva-bhūta-sthitaṁ yo māṁ bhajatyekatvam āsthitaḥ
sarvathā vartamāno 'pi sa yogī mayi vartate*

32

*ātmaupamyena sarvatra samaṁ paśhyati yo 'rjuna
sukhaṁ vā yadi vā duḥkhaṁ sa yogī paramo mataḥ*

33

arjuna uvācha
yo 'yaṁ yogas tvayā proktaḥ sāmyena madhusūdana
etasyāhaṁ na paśhyāmi chañchalatvāt sthitiṁ sthirām

34

chañchalaṁ hi manaḥ kṛiṣhṇa pramāthi balavad dṛiḍham
tasyāhaṁ nigrahaṁ manye vāyor iva su-duṣhkaram

35

śhrī bhagavān uvācha
asanśhayaṁ mahā-bāho mano durnigrahaṁ chalam
abhyāsena tu kaunteya vairāgyeṇa cha gṛihyate

36

asaṅyatātmanā yogo duṣhprāpa iti me matiḥ
vaśhyātmanā tu yatatā śhakyo 'vāptum upāyataḥ

37

arjuna uvācha
ayatiḥ śhraddhayopeto yogāch chalita-mānasaḥ
aprāpya yoga-sansiddhiṁ kāṅ gatiṁ kṛiṣhṇa gachchhati

38

kachchhin nobhaya-vibhraṣhṭaśh chhinnābhram iva naśhyati
apratiṣhṭho mahā-bāho vimūḍho brahmaṇaḥ pathi

39

etan me sanśhayaṁ kṛiṣhṇa chhettum arhasyaśheṣhataḥ
tvad-anyaḥ sanśhayasyāsya chhettā na hyupapadyate

40

śhrī bhagavān uvācha
pārtha naiveha nāmutra vināśhas tasya vidyate
na hi kalyāṇa-kṛit kaśchid durgatiṁ tāta gachchhati

41, 42

prāpya puṇya-kṛitāṁ lokān uṣhitvā śhāśhvatīḥ samāḥ
śhuchīnāṁ śhrīmatāṁ gehe yoga-bhraṣhṭo 'bhijāyate
atha vā yoginām eva kule bhavati dhīmatām
etad dhi durlabhataraṁ loke janma yad īdṛiśham

43

tatra taṁ buddhi-sanyogaṁ labhate paurva-dehikam
yatate cha tato bhūyaḥ sansiddhau kuru-nandana

44

pūrvābhyāsena tenaiva hriyate hyavaśho 'pi saḥ
jijñāsur api yogasya śhabda-brahmātivartate

45

prayatnād yatamānas tu yogī sanśhuddha-kilbiṣhaḥ
aneka-janma-sansiddhas tato yāti parāṁ gatim

46

*tapasvibhyo 'dhiko yogī
jñānibhyo 'pi mato 'dhikaḥ
karmibhyaśh chādhiko yogī
tasmād yogī bhavārjuna*

47

*yoginām api sarveṣhāṁ mad-gatenāntar-ātmanā
śhraddhāvān bhajate yo māṁ sa me yuktatamo mataḥ*

Contact

9839093003

myrichindia@gmail.com

facebook.com/drjagadeeshpillaiofficial

youtube.com/drjagadeeshpillai

www.ingramcontent.com/pod-product-compliance
Lightning Source LLC
Chambersburg PA
CBHW031513150726
47990CB00007B/3007